THE STORY OF US

by Mitali Perkins

illustrated by Kevin and Kristen Howdeshell

beaming ☀ books
MINNEAPOLIS

One day, Creator came—

to sort the mess,

using Them to make Us.

Air.
Water.
Earth.
Fire.

They were for Us.

We were for Them.

Breath takers—

Tag the breeze!

Thirst quenchers—

Dance with rain!

Soil tillers—

Play in mud!

Fire builders—

Tend the flames!

But—

We said: "No, Creator!"

We said: "No Creator."

And They, too, fell and changed.

Rose up, like monsters—

to fight Us.

Tornado.

Flood.

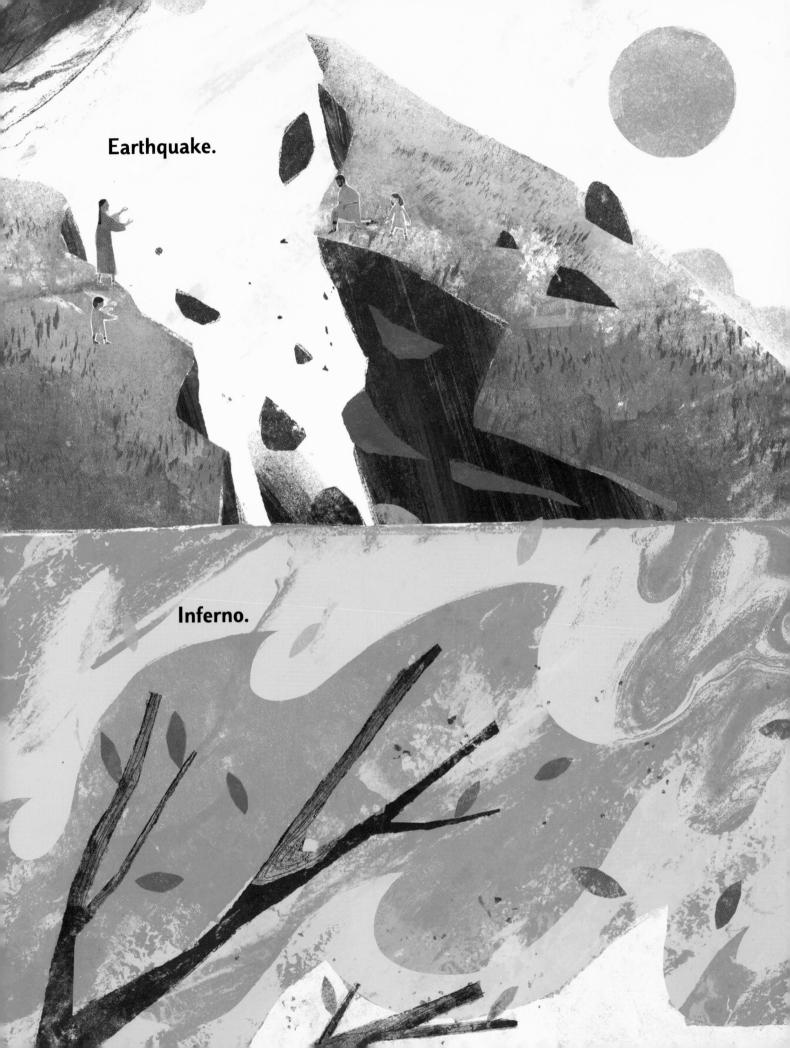

Earthquake.

Inferno.

We clawed back.

Greed.

Poison.

Waste.

Arson.

At war—

Them and Us.

One day, Redeemer came—

to change the mess,

using Them to serve Us.

Earth for blind eyes.

Water for tired feet.

Air to draw in a last breath—

and no more.

Until fire, for fuel,

fish on the shore.

One day, Restorer
came—

to end the mess,
bringing Them
close to Us.

Air for songs.

River, full of life.

Earth, clean and new.

Fire for gold.

At peace—

Them and Us.

For Carl and Rupali.
—M.P.

To the Somers family, we love you.
—K.H. & K.H.

Text copyright © 2022 Mitali Perkins

Illustrations copyright © 2022 Kevin Howdeshell and Kristen Howdeshell

Published in 2022 by Beaming Books, an imprint of 1517 Media. All rights reserved. No part of this book may be reproduced without the written permission of the publisher. Email copyright@1517.media. Printed in the United States of America.

28 27 26 25 24 23 22   1 2 3 4 5 6 7 8

Hardcover ISBN: 978-1-5064-8284-2

eBook ISBN: 978-1-5064-8285-9

Library of Congress Cataloging-in-Publication Data
Names: Perkins, Mitali, author. | Howdeshell, Kevin, illustrator. |
  Howdeshell, Kristen, illustrator.
Title: The story of us / by Mitali Perkins ; illustrated by Kevin and
  Kristen Howdeshell.
Description: Minneapolis : Beaming Books, 2022. | Audience: Ages 3-8 |
  Summary: "A lyrical exploration of the relationship between the natural
  elements, humanity, and God"-- Provided by publisher.
Identifiers: LCCN 2021049910 (print) | LCCN 2021049911 (ebook) | ISBN
  9781506482842 (hardcover) | ISBN 9781506482859 (ebook)
Subjects: LCSH: Creationism--Juvenile literature.
Classification: LCC BS651 .P444 2022 (print) | LCC BS651 (ebook) | DDC
  231.7/65--dc23/eng/20220126
LC record available at https://lccn.loc.gov/2021049910
LC ebook record available at https://lccn.loc.gov/2021049911

VN0004589; 9781506482842; JUL2022

Beaming Books
PO Box 1209
Minneapolis, MN 55440-1209
Beamingbooks.com